I AM

JUST A

GHOST

SHELBY EGNEW

MILTON & HUGO L.L.C.
4407 Park Ave., Suite 5
Union City, NJ 07087, USA

Website: *www. miltonandhugo.com*
Hotline: *1- 888-778-0033*
Email: *info@miltonandhugo.com*

Ordering Information:
Quantity sales. Special discounts are granted to corporations, associations, and other organizations. For more information on these discounts, please reach out to the publisher using the contact information provided above.

Library of Congress Control Number: 2024919956
ISBN-13:   979-8-89285-333-0   [Paperback Edition]
                 979-8-89285-334-7   [Digital Edition]

Rev. date: 09/25/2024

*for every person who picked themselves up
when no one could see them...*

Contents

I Am Just A Ghost

I am just a ghost,
always floating in and out,
of all the places in my life
that I'd forgotten all about.

Sometimes I'm there, sometimes I'm not,
Sometimes I wait for them to see me –
but most often they do not.

I watch them from the shadows,
as they go about their life,
making friends and lovers
while I hide them from my strife.

I don't know how it happened,
but I used to be like them.
Then one day I was gone
and knew I wasn't whole again.

I am just a shadow
of the things that used to be.
I wonder still, as life goes on,
if anyone remembers me.

Do they remember how I used to laugh?
And how I used to dream?
For though I wait here, haunting,
I'm not just what I seem.

I wish that I was real again -
that I remembered how to feel.
I'd write my story with a pen
and close it with a seal.

For some young soul who needs a tale
of love and loss too stormy
for this broken soul to sail.

Perhaps one day she'll need it
to move through the vicious gale.

For even if I'm not remembered,
I'd lose it all so she could walk,
home safely on the trail.

Myths & Legends

I was born to be a mermaid,
luring sailors to the sea.
Or a queen holding my court,
from the mountains to the lea.

Or a Scottish milkmaid dancing,
with ribbons in her hair.
Or an Italian noble posing,
for a portrait of the gods in air.

Maybe a pretty phantom,
walking 'cross the haunted moors.
I was born to be so many things
I've never been before.

I'd rather be a myth like these,
than be the one I have to be.
I hope in some bright sky,
I can be all I never was.
At that's what I pray to God above.

I m No Longer Pretty

I want to be a housewife,
with a home and perfect hair.
I want to wake my children,
with a loving, righteous air.

I want to be a housewife,
cooking fresh bread in the stove.
Keeping all our rooms clean,
bringing picnics to the grove.

I want to be a housewife,
with a set of pearls so fine.
Rings to give my daughters,
wisdom for the boys of mine.

I want to be a housewife,
and wait for my husband patiently.
We'll dance there in the kitchen,
and take vacations to the sea.

I want to be a housewife,
but it seems impossible.
My husband isn't here yet,
and children seem intangible.

I'm no longer pretty,
and I'm only growing old.
Fairy tales never told me,
how to walk a lonely road.

I want to be a housewife,
but it seems its not to be.
I'll just keep working all my life,
alone with only me.

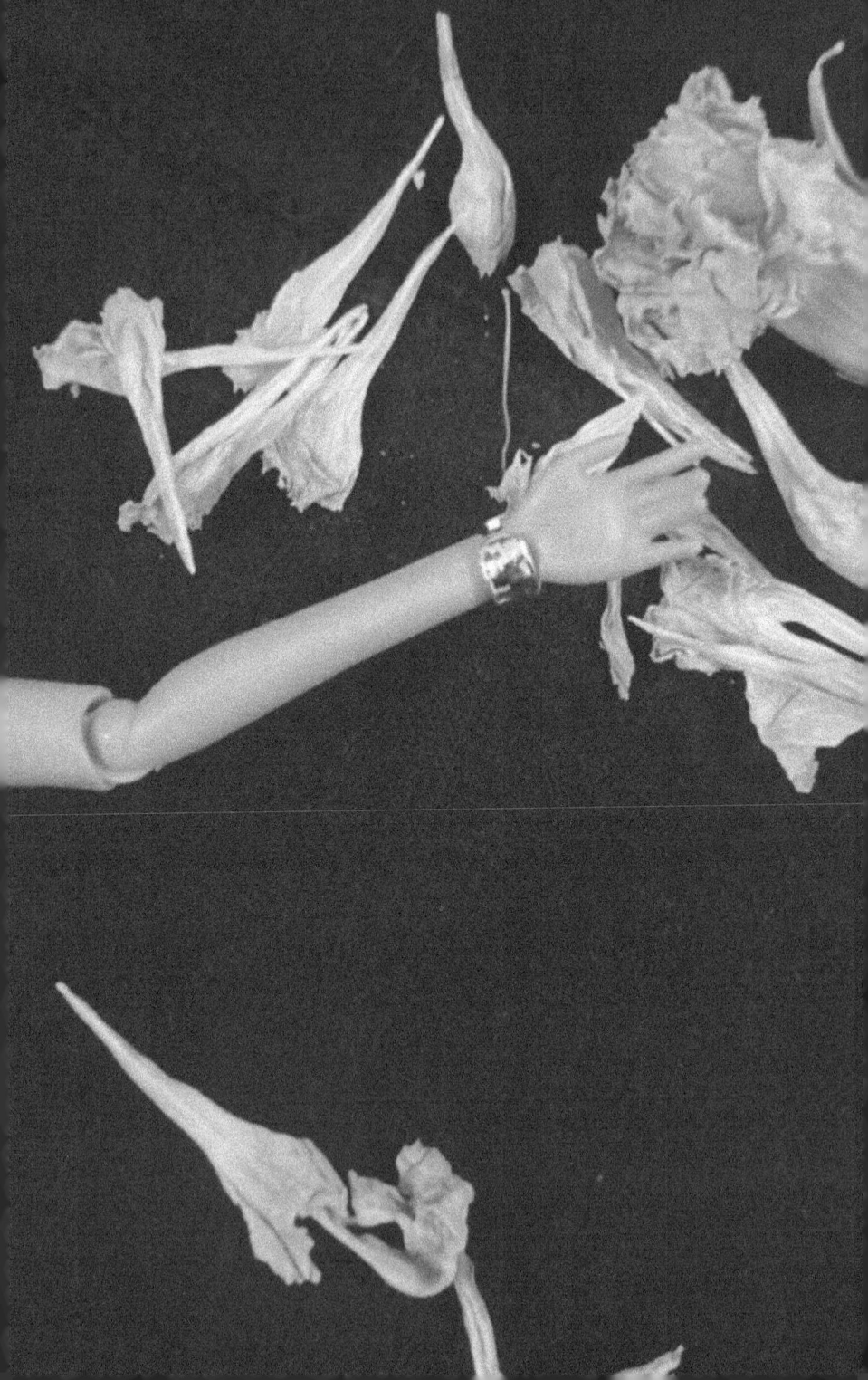

A Doll Upon A Shelf

It's been a year and I'm still here,
not much different than before.

My plans were many, but I didn't do any,
because how could they work out?

The people all around me wonder why I'm not myself,
but they don't know how it feels to be a doll upon a shelf.

Pull my string and I will sing – and dance-
to make you laugh.
But walk right past and I will just
sit here collecting dust.

When I was new, they all proclaimed –
what joy that I would bring.
How beautiful, how bright she is –
I love to hear her sing!

But when I got old, they stopped hearing
and they didn't say a thing.

I know my arm is wobbly and my face -
it has a crack.
But the silence sometimes feels
like being stretched upon a rack.

I did not know that getting older
would be like dying young.
People don't want a broken doll,
when all they see is songs unsung.

Stained Glass Windows

The window bathes the floor in prismatic pools of light.
To stand there savoring the color,
and take in the emulsion of fragmented pigments,
makes me ponder on the brokenness of each pane of glass.

I wonder if the tiny shards felt it as they shattered.
Did they know the hammer crushing them
would end in such a masterpiece?

How long did they wait to be placed into
exactly the right thread of the tapestry?
Did they trust the maker's hands?
I can see the bigger picture now, but I hope that they can too.

My place in the mosaic is still a mystery.
I am only small, like the blue piece at the bottom.
So tiny and unyielding.
Please, maker, I beg you truly,
don't forget to craft something for me.

Don't forget to give me space,
in the window frame of time.

Somewhere In The Universe

In another life, I still dance with pointe shoes,
in my leotard and tights.
In another life, I'm not alone,
on the cold and empty nights.

In another life, I'm a mother keeping house.
My children all are safe and real.
In another life, I'm happy,
with a father here and healed.

In another life, I had everything I needed.
I didn't have to break to bend.
In another life, I got to be loved and known
as more than just a friend.

But I don't get another life,
so, I can't waste any more time.
Wishing it was different -
instead of building what I want.
So, I guess I'll rise and make the bed,
and not surrender to my haunts.

A Hopeless Fool

There's this silly thing inside me -
it rises up like mist.
In spite of all the darkness,
it never does extinguish.

Everything seems impossible,
yet still it rises up.
I hope it's not in vain —
that the hope and dreams fly up.

I'm afraid it's all a trick —
delusion, foolish thoughts —
That it will only be for nothing
that I fight and carry on.

Sometimes I can't decide
if hope is good or bad.
If it makes it hurt,
or brings me joy I've never had.

My biggest fear is if I fight and struggle,
that I'll still run out of time.
And nothing will be left of me,
no legacy – no child of mine.

No one to remember
my favorite food or favorite song.
No one left to care about
the girl who carried on.

If it's all for nothing
then that is truly cruel.
Maybe all my hope and fight
is just me being a fool.

Can I Try Again?

I don't know what has happened to the world.
When I was small, it seemed so bright.
My heart was full of happy endings
and I didn't feel the night.

But now that I am older, the world I knew is gone.
The fairy tales I lived on are all crumbled into ash.
And I don't think I'm the hero,
I'm just begging for the past.

I don't know how I got here – to a world that makes no sense.
There used to be a safety in the four walls all around.
Now evil creeps into the corners and pushes in too fast.
I have to fight all day it seems - to cover cracks and keep it out.

It's like somehow, I got all mixed up -
living in the wrong timeline.
One where every fear comes true.
The worst of all the worst,
seem to shadow me like pine.

I don't know what has happened to the world.
And I don't know what's happening to me.
Give me back my childhood – maybe I can try again?
This wasn't how it's supposed to be.

I Am A Creature
Not Well Known

I am a creature not well known.
The self can be a mystery, sometimes even unknown to me.
Every day is a discovery of who I am or what might be.
The trouble is I don't always like it –
seeing all the parts of me.

I'm not sure what is left anymore.
I feel just like a shell.
Like all the shiny, golden pieces
crumbled into nothing as they fell.

My reflection in the mirror echoes back the dark.
My mother's grief, my father's anger.
Does God not think I'm good enough
to have all the things I want?

People only saw the good in me for just a little while.
When you get older and the grief does not subside,
people stop giving you grace.
They just look at you like you're the problem
for not being ok.

I wish that they could see past all my failures and my flaws,
how much my heart is longing to give love.
I want to live a life that's full -
but it seems I just don't have enough.

Give It Back

The forests are burned, and the flowers have died.
Planes overhead crashing, flaming pieces fall from skies.

Time has taken its captives, ripping holes through what should be.
Furious storms beat upon me like shattered bullets of glass.

Through the adventitious chaos, watchers stare,
adjudicating while I cry.
"Get up!" they seem to say.
"Why can't you do it? You're no good to me or anyone –
why don't you just lay down and die?"

Don't they see what's all around them?
My father gone, my brother too.
Please don't tell me to get up -
I don't think there is a point.

So tell me why should I?
And suddenly I understand
why children shout and cry.
"Give it back!" I scream into the void.
I only wanted what was mine.

The Faceless Man

I don't see him anymore -
the faceless man who lives in dreams.
He used to meet me in the dreamland
in the middle of the night.

He'd brush my cheek and tell me how I'm loved.
We raised children and built homes.
He would wake me from the bad dreams
and tell me I'd be fine.

Now he's vanished like the wind,
and still I search for him each night.
But I can't even reach him.
Why won't he come to see me?
Did I forget to do something right?

So my tears water the pillow,
for if he's not even in dreams,
then what wishes can I trust?

The Robot & Me

You know that machine trapped in a glass display case? It tries to clean up its own mess as spectators watch from the other side; their fingerprints smudging the window as they squish their noses trying to get a closer look. The blackish oil leaks out from the center of the machine as it tries endlessly to sweep it back in. No matter how hard it tries, the tiring efforts and aching mechanics never make a difference. I know it's just an art installation. It was designed that way. People come to watch and they feel sad for a little while. But then they get to go home and get back to their lives. Even if they have their own messes, they at least get to bury them under the rug. The machine's is bleeding, pouring out and splattering over the walls. It's an evisceration, an autopsy, a gutting. I think if I ever got to visit the bleeding machine, I would stand there as long as I could. Not to dawdle, not to gawk. To let it know that it is not alone. People have flesh and blood instead of gears and hydraulics. But our heart experiences the same. It groans and it yearns, and it heaves with effort as it tries to do what it can. It's usually never enough. But it beats and it tries, and it tries again. I'm not sure what it feels like anymore — to be the person on the other side of the glass — but I know how that lonely robot feels. Forever trying to fix what has always been too much — what was never in control in the first place — what can never be beautiful again. Locked in a glass box it can never invite anyone into. Forced to be a spectator's spectacle at the cost of everything it doesn't want to be seen as. Please, let someone rescue it. Please let someone rescue me.

I ve Been Looking
For My Father

I've been looking for my father –
have you seen him anywhere?
He has blue eyes, a darkened brow,
And thickened, chestnut hair.

They said he's dead and gone forever,
but I don't want to believe it.
I search in every face I know –
of my friends and family too.
Is that you there in those kind eyes?
Or are you somewhere out there listening
to my lonely, mournful cries?

Where are you, dad? Are you ok?
I know that you were hurting,
But I didn't think you'd leave so soon.
Was I not enough for you to stay?
I didn't know it was our last June.

I know I shouldn't want you
after all you put us through.
But I am quite forgiving – at least
to the man I thought was you.

But even if you weren't that man,
I'm still a girl who needs her dad.
If you're out there somewhere listening,
please hear me and come back.
Do what you need to do and then
maybe I won't have to be so sad.

I know I could face anything if I knew
that you were coming home to me.
Come back and we can try again
just you, daddy, and me.

I know that it's not real
and you are buried in the ground.
My children and grandchildren
won't remember you at all.
They won't even get to meet you,
since the gunshot made you fall.

But it was you who chose to leave me,
here to live life all alone.
So I guess I have to keep on searching,
for a father of my own.

My Life Is Like A Country Song

My life is like a country song.
(not the parties, beer and trucks)
The kind with failed romance, tragic tales,
and terrible bad luck.

Like the ones that echo through the hills
with ghost-like whines.
The ones that make you cry -
and also question why.

Unrequited love that never sees the light,
unmitigated rage at the hardships of our time.
Pretending all our ghosts aren't there,
looking down the barrels of guns
with cold, unfeeling stares.

A mystery unsolved, replayed with haunting melody.
The kind that makes you play it over and over.
Looking for the answer, but it's nowhere to be found.
My life is like a country song,
I have to keep on living, 'till I'm buried in the ground.

Grief Is Ugly

Grief has shattered me to pieces.
One cracked with my father
the other with my grandma,
one with someone I won't name.

I'm afraid of what is left now,
some snarling, wounded creature,
that's afraid to go outside.

It runs and hides away now,
biting when people get too close.
I don't why it does that -
that's not what I really want.

But I don't know how to change it
and make up for all the years of love
she was supposed to have.

Everyone says eventually it will get better,
but I don't think it will.
How do you glue back a mirror
obliterated by disappointed hopes?

Every time a piece has broken,
it permanently alters the frame.
Nothing is the same now
and can't ever be again.

The Fall Of Troy

I watched the fall of Troy last night,
from my seat upon the hill.
The city was engulfed in flames
that rose to skies of evil till –

the screams of all the dying
echoed long after the rain.
The place that once was golden
fell and ne'er will rise again.

How many times has history been erased
for the whims of prideful plans?
How many innocents must die
for the wounded ego of a man?

Helen was no villain,
Cassandra only tried to help,
Andromache merely wanted
a wife and mother so to be.

But still Helen lost her Paris -
they gave Cassandra to a monster.
Hector and her baby torn,
from Andromache's arms
that dreadful morn.

Seeing such destruction,
far from all ability to help,
makes one ponder on the passing
of our temporary days of time.

We're only ashes in the wind —
to dust we shall return.
But that dust once was beautiful.
Maybe that's the lesson we must learn.

My Own Worst Enemy

I am so alone that
I'm my own worst enemy.
No one else to turn to,
no one else to blame.

The clock is ticking onward,
28 is on its way.
I wonder if I'd feel it,
if I put my hand in flames.

Sometimes it just feels like
I am already dead.
What I used to fight for slipped
from horizons in my head.

These curses and these failings,
stone me like a martyr.
Sometimes it is easier
to let them hit me.

I look outward for a reason,
but none of them appear.
So it must be something wrong with me -
at least that is what I fear.

Silly Little Me

How silly of me to think that you'd care -
how wretched of me to say it's not fair.
I know – I know – there's no room for despair,
I should have known better than to hope you'd be there.

Heaven forbid that I trust you might listen.
It must be too much to ask, that you might see my vision.
The loneliest feeling is thinking in fiction -
with no one to hear me in my mind-confined prison.

How Are You? I m Fine.

My dreams are only specters,
battlefields strewn with corpses
of wasted desires.
Shadows of what might have been
waltzing under the moonlight.
Graveyards of opportunities passed on,
gardens of flowers withering on the vine.

My dreams are only specters,
phantoms of the starless night.
How much there could have been,
haunts the waking hours of the day.
The wrong petal has fallen,
curses laugh at me from pedestals.
So how can I say that I am fine?

The Wind Doth Blow

I worry if the wind blows hard,
that I'll just fly away.
I thought I was made of stronger stuff,
but life has made me fragile.

One tiny breath or wailing gust
and I may just
snuff out like candlelight.
Ripple away across the waves,
or disappear like dust.

A Fatherless Child

I weep whenever I hear of
lost little girls without their father.
For in my heart, I know each one,
knows the same despair as me.

We'll always be there watching
and waiting by the door.
We'll stand with all great diligence.
Though coming home – he will! – no more.

A daughter's love is constant,
lasting years of darkened nights.
But only if the father's careful –
can she stop it cracking all her sight.

It safeguards and it chastens.
It forgives and it hastens.
It twists and breaks and bends itself,
rather than placing him up on a shelf.

Cursed be the father that abuses
his daughter's tender heart.
For her love will haunt him always.
Her pleadings and her wailings -
he'll heed them if he's smart -

will blow across the earth,
till they find him in the end.
Wherever he is wandering
aimless 'cross the wasted wilds.
And maybe he'll come running back
to his wretched, waiting child.

She s Lost Her Bloom

My time has passed,
my bloom rubbed off,
golden years sped by.

It would not bother,
had they been of use,
but waste is wanton,
and it ravages away.

Every joyful youth, I envy,
and every blushing bride.
Time gave them banquets -

It only gave me crumbs,
leaving me grim and battle worn.

"One spent and weary soldier"
they whisper now, "is she."

I m A Childless Mother

I don't think I'll be complete,
till I hold a baby of my own.
With bright blue eyes
and tiny feet.

Right now, my womb is empty,
and my heart is inside out.
I hope they're not waiting for me -
I'm afraid I can't get out
of this darkness deep inside me.
I'll try to claw my way back out!

If I ever get a baby,
I would love them so intensely -
create a shield that stops all pain.
I'd have a reason to get up for -
a rainbow coming after rain.

I try so hard to be enough,
so one day a mother I can be.
But what if fear and sadness take me?
And my children, I'll not see?

CLIPPER DIARY 1937

DESK-AIDE 1940 ★

DAILY-AIDE 1944 ★

1950

Emily & Sylvia

I think I know why Emily Dickinson
didn't like to leave her room.
Why Sylvia wrote her sorrows
in a melancholy tune.
There's only so much we can handle,
way down here beneath the moon.

Not everyone is cursed to know,
this sorrow that runs deep.
A silent, numbing current that cuts
through all the secret hopes I keep.

Eventually the sorrow means,
you shut out what you can.
To ease a bit off of the edge,
ghost-like retreat is now my plan.

The Light Of Fireflies

There is nothing like the quiet
of a peaceful summer night.
No sound but the crickets,
at the fading of the light.

If only I could stay there -
in the light of fireflies.
Forever feeling warm and safe
from cold and painful lies.

My soul is tethered to the earth
in spring and summertime.
With sun and flowers blooming,
it leaps up with hope and thyme.

If the earth can die and live again,
then surely, I can too.
My winters and my dying leaves
won't always be my truth.

My life will grow in seasons,
always changing, never still.
Each one will never come again,
so I must love them all until,

one day when they are done and I
don't have a season left.
Then I'll look back at what I've made,
when persevering through the rest.

Summertime

A summer of waiting,
of staving off the inevitable
changes in flux.
Something is cooking under the hot and humid sun.

I can't tell what it is;
my deliverance or my doom.
Weaves of tangled messes
clutter up my mind.

I pick and choose which ones I can,
but if I handpick the wrong one,
the knots will never loosen.
There will be nowhere left to run.

No one knows what I'll do next
and neither, must I say, do I.
Directions don't seem to matter so,
when madness feels so high.

Rainwater

I collect words like rainwater. They are my greatest friends.
For, sometimes they can see me when other people don't.
To know that someone else – yesterday or long ago – could
string the pieces of my soul all together in a poem.
I'd really love to meet them, even though I know I
won't. We're separated by life and time and paper, but
yet I feel I know them, the author of those works.
If they can feel what I feel and put it to the pen, then maybe
somehow there is meaning in my struggle and my toil.
The words that comfort me will live on in my head
and maybe I'll write my own someday, to comfort
some poor soul – yes, I think that is the goal.
Yes, that's what I will do. My heart won't be so heavy,
my mind won't be so full, if I can give it to the pen and
page – adding my own raindrops to the bowl.

Two Little Cars

There's a driveway in my neighborhood,
with two Volkswagen bugs.
I want to be like them one day -
blue monograms with matching mugs.

The driveway all surrounded,
by blades of emerald green.
Mossy clover shades the earth and
tiny dandelions
make a whimsy fairy sheen.

The setting screams of magic,
mixed with family and with love.
The ancient and the modern
live together here above.

I bet it fits them perfectly,
the little family in their home.
My driveway now is lonely,
but one day, maybe less so.

Right now, I'm just beginning,
on the way to find my own.
Perhaps if I work hard enough,
I won't have to be alone.

Then in my driveway lying there,
we'll have two little cars.
Yours is grey and mine is green,
and we'll drive out to see the stars.

Car seats and vacations - and even tires too,
will cycle throughout all the years.
As we create a life of wonder
from the deluge of my lonely tears.

Hope Wrapped Up In Rhymes

I'm living in the sunsets,
in the flowers and the trees.
In the music and the laughter,
and the happy cry movies.

I may not be the loudest
or the best at everything.
But I'm in there — in those moments -
that make a sad heart sing.

The raindrops and the quiet
of a bluebird's pretty song.
The color of an ocean wave
and life lived well and long.

I may not have a trophy,
no perfect job or shiny hair.
But I have precious moments,
and I think that's more than fair.

Sometimes in the darkness
I think of all those times.
That light was singing to me,
like hope wrapped up in rhymes.

Footprints Of My Being

Haunting guitar, siren-like songs,
dusty old books and warm spring winds.
Lipstick on my paper cup,
vintage movies, tortured words.

Historic portraits, wild roaming hills,
ocean whitecaps, autumn leaves.
Times gone by, heartache threadbare,
echoes of pink pointe shoes,
stepping out their quiet dreams.

Strings of pearl, chlorine shimmer,
sunlight on my face, keeping out the cold.
Single flowers growing in a lonesome wilderness.

Hopeful nothings, tales untold,
the legends and the myths,
of countries green and old.
Twinkle lights and phthalo green.

The footprints of my being,
burned into the space between.

Hopeful Wishing Folk

Maybe my existence is to give dreams
to those who came before.
The hopeful wishing folk -
the ones whose dreams were never answered
and their prayers went up in smoke.

For though my hopes are pending,
there is beauty in a "no".
I don't have what I wanted,
but I still experience and grow.

My being is the dream
that many people want.
Though sometimes I give little,
I am witness to the earth.

All the things that haunt and sing,
the cries and joys of people,
that go on anyway.

And if I come to nothing,
it won't be all in vain.
Because I lived a little while
to triumph over pain.

Lighthouses In Dark Skies

I'm going to name my daughters
Lenora & Caroline,
named for my mother and grandmother,
who raised all of us so fine.

Little Lenny will be brave and wise,
as I know she'll need to be.
But I pray she's also happy,
finding joy in every sea.

Little Lina will be sweet and kind,
but strong enough to stand —
and face all of her battles
with a fierce and righteous hand.

I'll raise them on the squally shores
that Lina is named after.
Days under sun, nights under moon -
Lenny smiling in her sleep, as I say goodnight to her.

We'll weather all the hurricanes
and ride our currents of heartbreak.
I'll teach them all our history
and how to sail onward from mistakes.

They will grow into strong women –
much greater than plain I –
whose truth radiates outward
like lighthouses in dark skies.

If I get to meet them,
and my fairytale comes true -
then this is my incarnate melody.
If I don't get the chance,
I'll hold them in my heart with me.

We're alive somewhere on those shores,
knit as tight as tapestries.
Painting our own masterpiece,
of life, love and family.

This Body

If I weren't tethered to this body,
I would dance just like I used to.
Maybe so well that I would fly,
into the arms of my sweet Romeo,
lifting me with strong and steady hands.

If I weren't tethered to this body,
maybe men would still call me beautiful.
My limbs would feel like feathers,
and I wouldn't feel the need
to shrink myself into the smallest corners.

If I weren't tethered to this body,
I could travel everywhere.
To the mountains and the oceans all across the globe.
I wouldn't miss a single landscape -
every sunset could be mine.

If I weren't tethered to this body,
I could live a thousand lives.
Every dream of mine fulfilled,
each dance step falling at the perfect time.
Perfect rhythms, flowing lines, alluring rhyme.

A World War One Soldier

There's a WWI soldier standing guard
over Charlotte Avenue.
I pass him on my way to the stage.
"You don't know me," I think to myself, "but I know you."

I think your name is Alvin.
They called you up to fight.
You didn't really want to,
but duty won the day and night
as you fought through hell and back.

You shouted at the enemy,
to tell them to come down.
A soldier with humanity,
like so many who went down.

I hope this world we've built since then
is something that you wanted.
I'm afraid we've all lost sight of something
falling prey to what the enemies had taunted.

Thank you, Alvin, for your service -
for laying down your life and dreams,
so that I could be free.
I hope I'll fight my battles
with the same humility.
And leave the world a little better
than the combat I grew up in.

Women

Women are the watchers, waiters,
keeping vigil at death's door.
Women are the soldiers, fighters,
waging holy war.

Women are the knowledge seekers,
philosophies of brilliant minds.
Women are the comforters
of broken hearts in all mankind.

Women are the nurturers,
raising people up with care.
Women are the listeners,
hearing voices of the others,
who don't have a voice to share.

Women are creators,
adding beauty to the world.
Women are the healers, feelers,
who harvest lost and broken souls.

Women are protectors,
of the young and innocent.
Women are the brave ones,
when dark dreams are imminent.

There's no one else that
I would rather be,
than a woman in this world,
like the mighty ones I see.

Chasms In My Mind

I have so much to write, because my mind is made of canyons.
Chasms of thoughts with rivers that rush rapidly.
I scramble like an artist, swirling charcoal into image,
as quick as I can do it, before the depth of each one flees.

In the shelter of my mind, I visit places all quite often.
Empty wedding chapels sit, waiting for the missing bride.
Pages and pages of unheard nothings lie,
in old ravines where I can hide.

Some paths are trod and traveled, and some are not yet open.
The beauty of my mind is the unexplored I've yet to go in.
Symphonies and coliseums, wonders treasured, not yet spoken.
Masterpieces to create, my favorite dreams I picture knowing.

I Have An Artist's Soul

When they call me up to say,
who I am and what's my name.
I don't know how to put it, except for me to say,
"I have an artist's soul."
I have no skill for worldly things,
like income and achievement.
Just an eye for beauty everywhere and the bravery to feel it.
Then to help others see what I see – that is my only goal.
I want to sculpt an image with my paintbrush,
and write a portrait of my dreams.
I want to sing a thousand lullabies
to my photographs of seas.
I want to dance triumphant symphonies
and march out a pleasant tune.

There's so much for me to do and yet,
it's impossible to try.
For part of the dilemma,
is choosing how I'd like to fly.

Lover Girl <3

In the face of horror,
love became my favorite thing.
I seek it out in everything,
though finding it escapes me.

I don't think it's for me,
but it's everything I dream about.
Night and day I picture my wedding,
the flowers I would choose —
and most importantly, the groom.

He handles all my softness,
with a careful, tender grasp.
He handles all my nightmares
by chasing them away.

Such a beautiful picture
in my imagined memory.
The horror might have crushed me,
but at least I have the dream.

June s Bright Skies

"My favorite month is June." I said,
as we watched the fireflies.
The sunsets and the starlight -
never quite as beautiful
as the ones in June's bright skies.

The Thing About Death

The thing about death,
is it's not very loud.
It sneaks up on you
like a friend in a crowd.

The thing about death,
is it wins over time.
We always wish for more,
but he never gives us a dime.

The thing about death,
is it takes our loves like light.
It winks it out so softly,
like a candle in the night.

But the thing about death,
with all the sadness and pain,
is it brings us together,
to shoulder all the strain.

You see, the thing about death
is it brings in a circle,
of love and great care,
to scare away the dark and hurtful.

Not always, of course,
but just if you're lucky.
You'll see good rush in with bad,
and then death does not win, does he?

It may cheer for a while,
but it won't be for long.
Because our stories will go on,
even when our breath is gone.

So, the thing about death
is it's never just final.
For if we keep loving and living and dying,
we still go on in our loved ones left crying.

When Storms Pass

There comes a point for me,
when the worst has already happened,
and nothing left is fair.

So I sit and weep awhile -
for all the things I've fought for
that crumbled to thin air.

Parts of me died with them,
and they're never coming back,
but maybe some things are still there.

In spite of all the anger,
fear and worry that I feel,
it seems like something's settled.

Like the moment when the storm clears,
dust storms fall and clouds are parted,
rocks are turned to precious metals.

Because when the worst has happened,
and somehow I survive it,
life renews like phoenix wings.

I discover I am stronger
than the storm that pulled me down.
My mending heart begins to sing.

A Gasp Of Air

I think I'm getting closer to the girl I'm meant to be.
I still get lost and very sad.
But every now and then I get a glimpse,
of what it feels like to be free.

Free from broken hopes and dreams;
the burdens of my being.
I hope I'll have the courage
to let bad things fall away.

To stop my pride from bristling,
and fear from being in control.
Instead of holding on so tightly,
I learn to breathe and let it go.

A Friend Who s Cold
And Silent

I love a friend who's cold and silent -
she never says a thing.
She lets me bleed all over her
and never says it's unfeeling.

She cannot wrap her arms around me,
or brush my tangled hair.
But she can hold all of my sorrow,
when all I say is "it's not fair".

No one knows her now,
for I keep her locked away.
Until one day a soul has earned it -
a glimpse of both of us at play.

"Who is she?" you are asking.
I guess perhaps that I can say.
She is my paper and my pen,
that I write upon today.

Life Goes On

In spite of all the horror-
grief unfurling through the floor -
Life goes on in droves,
sprouting up in groves.
It is such a thing of beauty
I just keep wanting more.

Dear Little One

To the one who once was me,

I wish that I could tell you everything would be alright.
The dreams we dreamed together didn't
make it through the night.
You probably would hate me and despise the reasons why I cry.
But still, in spite of all the pain, I will not say goodbye.

For though I cannot save you from the roadblocks up ahead,
on the other side of storm clouds, I can feel that you're not dead.
It was I who lost your loveliness and drove you to the ground,
but it will be me who lifts you up again and will not stop till
you are found.

I'm sorry for the heartaches and the lessons coming up.
I'll hold your hand through all of it and always fill your cup.
My love, just keep on dreaming, for this won't be our end.
And who knows what new dreams and hopes
will be coming forward round' the bend.

Sincerely,
Me

www.ingramcontent.com/pod-product-compliance
Lightning Source LLC
Chambersburg PA
CBHW032053040426
42449CB00007B/1089